Table of Contents

The Coping Deficit:

How Overprotection Broke Resilience

By Jennifer Topping

First Edition 2025

"For my loving and supportive husband & family and all of the conversations we've had over the years."

Introduction: The Era of Emotional Overload

There has never been a generation of parents more concerned about their children's happiness, safety, and emotional well-being than today's. Most of us grew up hearing phrases like "life's not fair" or "you'll be fine." Now, we find ourselves raising children in a world where fairness and feelings seem to outweigh nearly everything else.

Our culture has done a remarkable job of teaching empathy, awareness, and self-expression—but somewhere along the way, we lost balance. In our effort to protect our children from pain, disappointment, and failure, we may have unintentionally protected them from growth.

Psychology and parenting philosophies over the last few decades have placed enormous value on children's emotions—sometimes so much that feelings now dictate reality. When a child feels left out, uncomfortable, or unhappy, many adults rush to fix the situation rather than teach the child to face and manage it. The instinct comes from love and care, but the result is that many young people are entering adulthood with very few tools to handle life's inevitable hardships.

We've raised children who are emotionally literate but emotionally fragile—quick to name what they feel, but unsure what to do with it.

This book isn't about blaming parents, teachers, or even the influence of modern psychology. It's about understanding how good intentions led to unexpected consequences, and more importantly, how we can restore resilience, self-reliance, and healthy coping skills without losing empathy or compassion.

The Balance We Lost

Children need both comfort and challenge. They need to feel loved, but they also need to learn that not every feeling demands action from the world around them. Disappointment, rejection, and discomfort are not signs that something is wrong—they're part of the human experience. They build strength, patience, and adaptability.

When we remove every obstacle, soften every fall, or intervene at every moment of frustration, we prevent our children from discovering one of life's most valuable truths: they are capable of recovering on their own.

✦ ✦ ✦

What This Book Offers

Throughout this book, we'll explore how the cultural pendulum swung from tough love to overprotection, and how that shift has affected children's mental and emotional development. We'll look at why competition and conflict are essential, why the fear of "hurting feelings" has silenced honesty, and how the rise of cancel culture connects to a deeper fear of discomfort.

Most importantly, this book will offer practical ways for parents and teens to rebuild resilience— through everyday moments, conversations, and choices that teach balance, strength, and humility.

You'll find encouragement here, not guilt. You'll see explanations, not accusations. The goal isn't to go backward to harsher times, but to move

3

forward with wiser balance: empathy paired with endurance, and care paired with courage.

Because the truth is simple: children who never learn to cope with life's small struggles will one day crumble under its bigger ones.

But when we teach them how to feel and how to endure, we give them something much stronger than comfort.

We give them resilience.

Chapter 1: The Psychology Pendulum

From Awareness to Overprotection

Every generation of parents wants to do better than the last. After decades of "children should be seen and not heard," society rightly began paying attention to the emotional world of young people. Starting in the 1980s and 1990s, psychology and education began focusing on feelings—helping children understand, express, and name their emotions rather than suppressing them.

This was progress. We learned that children thrive in emotionally safe environments and that mental health matters. Schools started teaching emotional literacy, counselors encouraged self-expression, and parenting advice emphasized listening, validating, and protecting.

But like many cultural movements that begin with good intentions, the pendulum didn't stop in the middle. It swung too far.

In our quest to protect children's mental health, we began protecting them from mental challenge. We stopped letting them experience the very discomfort that develops strength, perspective, and maturity.

The Rise of "I'm Offended"

As emotional awareness grew, so did the idea that feeling hurt means something harmful has occurred.

This shift has shaped a generation that interprets discomfort as danger, and disagreement as disrespect. The phrase "I'm offended" has become both a shield and a sword—an automatic way to stop conversation rather than continue it.

When we teach children that every unpleasant emotion must be avoided, we unintentionally teach them that the world should change to fit their comfort level. That's not resilience—it's emotional dependency.

Feeling offended isn't a flaw; it's a signal that something doesn't align with our values or beliefs. But learning to tolerate that feeling—

without trying to silence or erase the source—is where emotional growth begins. Children who are constantly shielded from offense never learn to separate their feelings from the facts of life around them.

The Disconnected Perspective

This overemphasis on self-focus has created what psychologists now call a disassociated viewpoint: the inability to see beyond one's personal feelings or experiences.

Instead of learning, "I feel upset, but maybe someone else sees it differently," many young people now conclude, "If I feel upset, that means something bad happened, and someone else is wrong."

This emotional logic turns personal discomfort into moral judgment—and it's spreading throughout schools, social media, and public life. It's why a growing number of teens and young adults struggle to have civil discussions, tolerate opposing ideas, or simply coexist with difference.

The irony is brutal - the more we obsess over validating feelings, the less equipped people seem to be at actually understanding anyone else's. And, the less we learn to empathize.

The Cost of Constant Comfort

Children who never experience discomfort in safe, small doses—losing a game, being teased, feeling excluded, facing a tough teacher—miss out on crucial emotional training. Those moments teach perspective: how to manage frustration, interpret intent, and recover gracefully.

When adults rush to fix every problem, remove every obstacle, or step in at the first sign of distress, they unknowingly send the message:

"You can't handle this on your own."

Over time, children internalize that belief. The result is not confidence but fragility—an expectation that life should bend to their emotions.

Finding the Middle Again

The goal is not to swing back to emotional neglect or to dismiss feelings as weakness. It's to rebalance—to pair emotional understanding with accountability and tolerance.

We can teach our children that feelings are real but not always right; that emotions are signals, not commands. We can show them that it's possible to disagree without disrespect, to be offended without demanding silence, and to coexist with ideas that make us uncomfortable.

True mental strength doesn't come from avoiding distress—it comes from learning to navigate it.

As parents, teachers, and mentors, we have an opportunity to correct the pendulum's swing. Not by toughening our children in cold ways, but by trusting them to handle life's challenges with guidance instead of rescue.

Because one day, they won't have someone there to fix every hurt.

But if they've learned how to process, adapt, and keep going—they'll be more than fine.

They'll be strong.

Chapter 2: The Death of Losing

When Winning Became the Only Acceptable Outcome

No parent enjoys seeing their child lose. Whether it's a game, a grade, or a friendship, watching them struggle tugs at the deepest protective instinct we have. But somewhere over the last few decades, protecting children's self-esteem began to replace teaching them self-respect.

We began rewarding effort equally to outcome—not to encourage persistence, but to shield children from disappointment. The result was the rise of the participation trophy—a symbol of good intentions that quietly rewrote how children understand effort, achievement, and resilience.

Children stopped learning how to fail safely. And when losing feels like a crisis, not a lesson, we create young people who give up, blame others, or crumble under pressure rather than regroup and try again.

The Essential Skill of Losing

Losing—whether it's a soccer game, a debate, or a dream college—isn't a setback; it's a rehearsal for life. It teaches patience, humility, emotional regulation, and most importantly, perspective.

When we allow our children to experience and reflect on loss, they develop critical questions that lead to growth:

"What could I do differently next time?"

"What did I learn about myself?"

"How can I handle this feeling without giving up?"

Without those experiences, a child never learns the difference between failing and being a failure.

A small loss in childhood prepares them for bigger disappointments later—rejection, job competition, or heartbreak. If we remove every opportunity for frustration early on, adulthood hits like a brick wall.

The Discomfort Deficit

Modern childhood often lacks ordinary discomfort. Recess games without winners or losers, sports teams that "rotate" every player to keep things fair, schools that avoid grades or public recognition—these practices are meant to protect feelings. Yet they also remove opportunities for children to practice frustration, perseverance, and recovery.

Resilience isn't built through comfort; it's built through manageable stress. Just as muscles need resistance to grow, children need mild struggle to develop strength.

When life becomes too safe, children become too fragile.

From Growth to Fragility

Today, many young people interpret any failure as a reflection of personal inadequacy, not an opportunity for improvement. Some respond with anxiety or avoidance: "If I can't be the best, I won't even try." Others externalize the problem— blaming teachers, coaches, or systems rather than examining their own effort.

This isn't a character flaw; it's a learned mindset. When adults rush to rescue children from discomfort, they reinforce the idea that discomfort is intolerable. Over time, that belief becomes part of how the child sees the world: unfair, uncaring, and too hard.

Practical Ways to Reintroduce Losing and Learning

Parents and teachers can reverse this pattern gently and effectively. Here are a few simple but powerful ways to do it:

Let disappointment breathe.

When your child loses or fails, resist the urge to minimize it. Instead of "It doesn't matter," say, "I know that stings. Let's talk about what you learned."

Model healthy recovery.

Share your own moments of loss—missed opportunities, rejections, mistakes—and how you handled them. Show that adults lose too, and still keep going.

Encourage effort, not perfection.

Praise persistence, not just outcome. "I'm proud of how you handled that," means more than "I'm proud that you won."

Don't fix it—guide it.

When your child comes home upset, instead of calling the teacher or coach, help them come up with their own next step. Empowerment builds confidence faster than protection.

Reframe failure as feedback.
Teach that losing isn't the opposite of success— it's part of it. The ability to evaluate, adjust, and try again is the foundation of resilience.

Restoring the Value of the Struggle

When children learn that effort and outcome are connected—that trying hard sometimes still means losing—they develop patience, humility, and perspective.

The discomfort of losing becomes a teacher, not a trauma. And when they realize that they can survive that feeling, they start to approach life with courage instead of fear.

The truth is, the goal of parenting isn't to make our children comfortable—it's to make them capable.

Because the child who learns to handle loss with grace, effort, and humor will never truly lose.

They'll always find a way to grow.

Chapter 3: The Victim Mindset

When Every Hurt Becomes Harm

Somewhere along the line, we began confusing being hurt with being harmed.

Modern culture has grown increasingly sensitive to emotional pain — and while awareness of mental health is progress, overusing the language of trauma and victimhood has blurred the lines between real injury and ordinary hardship.

A child excluded from a group, corrected by a teacher, or teased by a classmate may now hear words like toxic, abusive, or unsafe applied to what are, in most cases, normal parts of growing up. These labels are not malicious; they come from a desire to validate feelings and protect children. But they also plant a dangerous idea:

"If something hurts, it must be wrong — and someone else is to blame."

This mindset discourages self-reflection and problem-solving, replacing them with blame and avoidance. It's the opposite of resilience.

How the Victim Mindset Develops

The victim mindset rarely begins as manipulation or laziness. It begins as protection. When adults constantly step in to defend a child from discomfort — from losing, being criticized, or feeling left out — the child learns that their emotions should control the situation.

Over time, the lesson becomes:

"If I feel bad, someone else caused it."

"If I'm upset, something unfair happened."

"If I'm offended, I deserve correction — not reflection."

It's a subtle shift from How can I handle this? to Who should fix this for me?

Unfortunately, this kind of thinking robs children of their sense of accountability and autonomy. Instead of developing self-responsibility, they develop emotional dependency — needing others to regulate, validate, or change things for them. They begin to see themselves as victims and, as victims, someone else must always be the perpetrator.

The Language of Fragility

Words matter. When we use terms like trauma, unsafe, or triggered to describe minor discomforts, we expand their meanings until they lose their seriousness.

True trauma — abuse, violence, or catastrophic loss — is life-altering and deserves professional support. But calling a disagreement or an unpleasant opinion "traumatic" dilutes compassion for those truly suffering. It also convinces others to see themselves as victims and lead them to believe that they're too fragile to cope with ordinary life.

The language of fragility shapes identity. When a young person repeatedly hears that they are a victim — of their peers, their school, or the system — they start to see themselves as powerless. And people who see themselves as powerless rarely grow stronger. Over time, they may also discover that the roll of victim can bring attention, sympathy, validation and lowered expectations.

The Power of Perspective

A healthy emotional life depends on proportion. Children need help learning that pain, frustration, and even unfairness can exist without defining them.

Being excluded once doesn't mean they're unloved.

Being criticized doesn't mean they're unworthy.

Being offended doesn't mean they're unsafe.

When adults model perspective — by saying things like, "That sounds painful, but you can handle it," or "Let's think about why that happened and what to do next" — we help children see themselves as active participants in life, not passive victims of it.

Perspective doesn't erase feelings; it puts them in context. And context builds coping skills.

From Blame to Growth

One of the hardest yet most important lessons we can teach is that unfair things happen — and not all of them need fixing. Sometimes, the best response is growth.

Instead of "Why did this happen to me?"

Try: "What can I learn from this?"

Instead of "They hurt me; I can't forgive them."

Try: "They hurt me, but I won't let it control me."

These are lessons in emotional ownership. They teach children that while they can't always control what happens, they can control how they respond. And that response is where true power lies.

Helping Children Build Resilience Instead of Victimhood

Parents can help reverse the victim mindset by practicing a few key habits:

Acknowledge feelings, but focus on solutions. Empathy matters. "That sounds tough" should always come before "What do you think you can do about it?"

Model accountability.
When adults admit mistakes, and show how they recover, children learn that strength isn't about never failing — it's about never staying stuck.

Avoid rescuing too quickly.
Let children struggle with small challenges. The discomfort they face now is emotional "training weight" for the future.

Use empowering language.
Replace "You poor thing" with "You're strong enough to get through this." Words shape identity.

Celebrate recovery, not avoidance.
Praise moments when your child worked through a problem — not when they escaped it.

The Return to Responsibility

Resilience and victimhood can't live in the same space. One takes ownership; the other gives it away.

We can teach our children that strength and empathy coexist — that they can feel deeply and still move forward, that acknowledging pain doesn't mean surrendering to it.

Because the truth is, life will not always be fair, kind, or gentle. But if we raise children who see themselves as capable rather than broken, they'll meet those moments not with outrage or despair, but with courage and perspective.

And that's the foundation of real strength.

Chapter 4: The Cancel Culture Connection

When Disagreement Became Dangerous

It used to be that disagreement sparked curiosity — "Why do you think that?"

Today, disagreement doesn't just spark conflict, it often incites condemnation — "How could you think that?" Or, "If you think that, you're the problem or the enemy."

This cultural shift didn't happen overnight. It's the natural extension of years spent teaching children that emotional discomfort is intolerable. When feelings become the measure of right and wrong, the moment something feels bad or offensive, it's seen as something that must be stopped.

At first glance, this seems protective: we don't want anyone to feel hurt or targeted. But when emotional safety replaces intellectual challenge, we end up with a culture that values comfort over truth, silence over growth and intolerance over difference.

The Roots of Cancel Culture

The modern "cancel" phenomenon — where people, books, movies, or even opinions are rejected and erased for being offensive — stems from the same overprotective mindset that shaped today's fragile resilience.

If children grow up believing that unpleasant feelings should be avoided, it follows that unpleasant ideas should be eliminated.

At its core, cancel culture is emotional reasoning in action:

"If it makes me uncomfortable, it must be wrong."

"If it offends me, it shouldn't exist."

This way of thinking removes personal responsibility and replaces it with moral authority. Rather than developing tolerance for different viewpoints, people learn to control the environment so they never have to experience discomfort at all.

Ironically, the more we try to make the world emotionally safe, the less emotionally safe it becomes — because everyone's threshold for offense keeps shrinking.

The Loss of Perspective

Cancel culture teaches emotional absolutism — the idea that our personal feelings define universal truth.

But truth isn't fragile, and disagreement isn't hate.

When children (and adults) lose the ability to separate emotion from evaluation, dialogue disappears. Instead of asking "Why do you believe that?" they jump to "You shouldn't believe that."

It's a mindset rooted in fear — fear of discomfort, of being wrong, or of being judged. But growth only happens when we can sit with that fear long enough to understand it.

We can disagree deeply and still respect one another. We can feel uncomfortable and still learn something valuable.

That's how societies — and individuals — evolve.

The Emotional Economy of Attention

Social media has amplified this cycle. Online, outrage is rewarded — every expression of offense attracts validation, clicks, and sympathy. It's a kind of emotional currency: the more hurt we appear, the more moral weight our words carry.

For teens, especially, this can become addictive. Expressing offense feels powerful; it signals identity, belonging, and control. But it's a false sense of empowerment. Instead of building confidence through reflection, they build it through rejection.

Real strength doesn't come from silencing others. It comes from knowing you can listen, think, and still stand firmly in your own beliefs.

Teaching Emotional Tolerance

Parents and teachers can begin reversing this trend in small but meaningful ways. Emotional tolerance — the ability to stay calm, curious, and kind in the presence of discomfort — can and must be practiced.

Here are some examples:

Encourage curiosity over correction.
When a child hears something they disagree with, teach them to ask questions instead of reacting.

"Why do you think that?" is far more powerful than "That's wrong."

Differentiate between discomfort and danger.
Not every upsetting statement is harmful. Help children recognize when they are truly unsafe — and when they're simply challenged.

Model calm disagreement.
Let your child see you handle opposing views with patience, not anger. Adults set the emotional tone that children mirror later in life.

Expose them to diversity of thought.
Read books, watch films, or discuss ideas that represent different sides. Teach that empathy doesn't mean agreement — it means understanding.

Reinforce identity through confidence, not control.
Help teens understand that their values are strong enough to withstand disagreement. A confident person doesn't need the world to agree with them.

The Strength of Staying Open

The healthiest minds are not the ones that avoid discomfort, but the ones that endure it thoughtfully.

When children learn that ideas themselves are not dangerous — that words can be examined, not feared — they develop the confidence to think critically and compassionately.

In the end, cancel culture isn't just about censorship; it's about fear of feeling and intolerance of differing ideas.

The antidote isn't outrage in the opposite direction — it's calm resilience.

We can raise a generation that doesn't shut down conversation but invites it.

One that doesn't silence discomfort but learns from it.

Because emotional maturity isn't found in protecting our feelings — it's found in expanding our capacity to face them.

Chapter 5: Parenting and Teaching for Strength

How to Build Resilience Without Losing Compassion

We all want our children to feel loved, valued, and emotionally secure. Those instincts are not the problem — they are the foundation of healthy parenting. The challenge is in how we define security.

True security doesn't come from removing every threat or soothing every frustration. It comes from helping children discover that they can face those challenges and survive them. A child who learns that they can handle discomfort becomes confident; a child who is always shielded from it becomes dependent.

This chapter is about restoring balance — blending empathy with endurance, validation with accountability, and love with limits.

1. The Role of Empathy: Listening Without Indulging

Empathy is powerful. When a child feels heard, they calm down; when they feel dismissed, they shut down. But empathy doesn't mean agreement, and it doesn't mean surrendering to emotion.

Too often, adults confuse "I understand" with "You're right." But it's possible — and essential — to separate the two.

When a child says, "It's not fair that I lost," an empathetic response might be:

"I know that's disappointing. You worked hard, and it hurts to lose."

Then, follow with perspective:

"But losing doesn't mean you failed. It means you have another chance to get better."

This approach validates the feeling without endorsing the conclusion. It shows love while still teaching logic.

2. The Value of Struggle: Letting Children Feel the Friction

Growth requires friction. Whether it's learning to share toys, face a tough subject, or navigate friendship drama, children gain strength by encountering small doses of frustration.

When adults rush to fix, comfort, or intervene, they unintentionally send the message that struggle is abnormal — or worse, that the child can't handle it. But when adults step back just enough, children discover their own coping tools.

A few examples:

When your child forgets their homework, resist bringing it to school. Let them experience the consequence, then talk about what to do differently.

When they're upset about a friend, don't immediately call the other parent. Ask, "How do you want to handle this?"

When they say, "I can't do it," respond with, "Try once more — I'll help if you really need it."

Each of these moments says: I believe you can handle this. That belief becomes self-belief.

3. The Power of Limits

Boundaries aren't punishment; they're structure. Children often interpret limits as love because they signal care, consistency, and stability.

A child who hears "no" and survives learns patience, self-control, and perspective. A child who never hears "no" learns that discomfort means danger — and will later struggle with authority, discipline, and self-restraint.

Set limits calmly and consistently. Instead of reacting emotionally, use reason:

"I know you're upset that we're leaving the park, but we made an agreement. We'll come back another day."

Boundaries are not barriers; they are training wheels for life.

4. Modeling Resilience

Children watch how we handle failure more than they listen to what we say about it. Every time we lose our temper, complain about being busy, or avoid uncomfortable situations, we're teaching emotional habits.

When we instead show calm recovery —
admitting mistakes, apologizing, laughing off
small setbacks — we give children permission to
do the same.

Let them see you mess up and bounce back. Say
things like:

"I'm frustrated right now, but I'll calm down and
try again."

"That didn't go as planned, but I learned
something."

Resilient children usually come from resilient
adults — not perfect ones.

5. Teaching Problem-Solving Instead of Protection

Children who can solve problems on their own
develop confidence that no compliment can
match. The best way to teach this is through
guided questioning.

When they face a challenge, ask:

"What do you think might help?"

"Have you felt this way before? What worked last
time?"

"If your friend were in this situation, what would you tell them?"

This process helps them move from emotion to reflection, from helplessness to strategy.

The goal isn't to have every answer — it's to help them find their own.

6. Strength Through Service

One of the most overlooked ways to build resilience is to teach empathy outwardly. Children who serve others — through volunteering, helping neighbors, or simply showing kindness — develop gratitude and perspective.

Service shifts the focus from "What's happening to me?" to "How can I help?"

It reminds them that their challenges, while real, exist in a larger world where everyone faces something. Gratitude is one of the strongest buffers against self-centeredness and victimhood.

7. Teaching the Language of Strength

The words we use shape the way children think about adversity. Replace fragile language with empowering alternatives:

Fragile Response	Resilient Alternative
"I can't do this"	*"This is hard, but I'll figure it out."*
"That's not fair."	*"Life isn't always fair, but I can adjust."*
"They were mean to me."	*"That hurt, but I can choose how to respond."*
I'm scared."	*"I'm nervous, but I'll try anyway."*

8. Resilience Is Love in Action

Empathy comforts; resilience empowers. The healthiest form of love combines both.

When we protect our children from every storm, they may stay dry for now — but they never learn to sail. When we walk beside them through the storm, teaching them how to steer, they grow strong enough to face anything life brings.

Strength doesn't mean suppressing emotion; it means understanding that emotions are temporary and survivable. And the most loving thing we can do is to help our children believe that truth for themselves.

Chapter 6: Building the Next Resilient Generation

Restoring Balance Between Compassion and Consequence

Every generation reshapes the world it inherits. Ours has brought extraordinary awareness to mental health, inclusion, and emotional safety — but in doing so, we've sometimes mistaken protection for progress. The good news is: we can correct course without abandoning care.

We don't need to return to the cold "toughen up" methods of the past. We just need to bring accountability back to stand beside empathy. Because without accountability, empathy collapses into enabling.

The Lost Connection Between Choice and Consequence

One of the most damaging cultural shifts of recent years is the erosion of consequence.

When a child misbehaves, struggles, or lashes out, too often the response is to explain rather than address. We label, rationalize, or excuse behavior — calling it anxiety, overwhelm, or "a bad day" — without teaching that feelings explain actions, but never excuse them.

Compassion should lead to understanding,

but understanding should always lead back to responsibility.

Children learn accountability through repetition: through small, consistent cause-and-effect lessons that show them their actions matter. When we remove those lessons to spare feelings, we create confusion — and confusion breeds entitlement.

Accountability is not punishment. It's guidance. It says, "Your choices shape your world." And that truth, though sometimes uncomfortable, is deeply empowering.

Why Excuses Weaken, but Ownership Strengthens

When we label every negative behavior instead of correcting it — "He's just sensitive," "She's overwhelmed," "They can't help it" — we tell children they have no control over themselves.

That strips them of dignity. It's not love to lower the bar; it's love to teach that they can rise to meet it.

Excuses might bring short-term comfort, but they create long-term helplessness. Ownership, on the other hand, restores strength. A child who learns to say, "I made a mistake, and I can fix it," is a child who will thrive anywhere.

Courage Over Comfort

Resilient people are not unfeeling — they simply understand that discomfort is part of growth. If we want to raise stronger children, we must give them opportunities to experience struggle safely, recover from mistakes, and see that they can survive hard things.

That means:

Letting grades reflect performance, not effort alone.

Allowing discipline to teach responsibility, not shame.

Encouraging dialogue instead of instant cancellation when someone says something offensive.

We need to move from "make everyone comfortable" to "help everyone capable."

Schools, Homes, and Communities as Partners

Resilience can't be built in isolation — it's a community project.

Schools can help by rewarding character as much as achievement, allowing room for productive failure, and creating environments that teach emotional regulation and accountability.

Parents can model resilience at home by maintaining boundaries, using consequences that teach rather than punish, and letting children earn back trust through changed behavior.

Communities can promote mentorship, service, and programs that connect youth with real-world challenge — not just comfort.

When the message is consistent across all these environments — that feelings are valid, but actions still have outcomes — children begin to internalize self-discipline, respect, and empathy that lasts a lifetime.

Restoring a Culture of Character

The ultimate goal isn't to create children who never hurt, fail, or offend. It's to raise people who can face those moments with integrity.

A healthy society doesn't silence mistakes; it learns from them. It doesn't cancel imperfection; it calls for growth. It doesn't hand out endless excuses; it hands out second chances with lessons attached.

If we can return to that balance — compassion with consequence, empathy with endurance — we'll raise a generation that's not fragile, not cruel, but strong and kind.

A Hopeful Future

Resilience isn't a lost art; it's a forgotten practice. It's built one small challenge at a time — one parent choosing to let a child fail safely, one teacher allowing honest discussion, one community valuing responsibility over reaction.

When we teach children that actions have consequences, that discomfort is temporary, and that strength and kindness can coexist, we don't just raise better kids — we build a better future.

Because the next resilient generation won't come from avoiding pain, but from facing it with courage, wisdom, and heart.

✦ ✦ ✦

Chapter 7 – When Words Become Walls

Language shapes culture, and culture shapes the way we think and feel. Over the past few decades, the idea of political correctness began with a noble goal: to encourage compassion in communication, to replace harmful stereotypes and cruel language with words that reflect respect and equality. It was never meant to silence people—it was meant to make kindness the norm.

But somewhere along the way, the pendulum swung again. What started as a guide for empathy has, in some places, turned into a rulebook for avoidance. Instead of promoting understanding, extreme political correctness can discourage open conversation altogether. People stop speaking not because they've learned respect, but because they've learned fear—fear of saying the wrong thing, fear of being labeled, fear of being misunderstood.

Children and teens absorb this climate quickly. In classrooms and online, they watch adults tiptoe through conversations, editing their words in real time, worried that even good intentions might offend. They learn that silence feels safer than expression, and comfort replaces curiosity. In this world, dialogue doesn't deepen—it disappears.

The unintended result is emotional fragility disguised as moral progress. When every opinion must be perfectly worded before it can be spoken, we lose the ability to practice tolerance, patience, and forgiveness. Disagreement begins to feel like disrespect, and correction feels like cruelty. Instead of learning how to cope with difference, young people learn to retreat from it.

The healthiest societies, like the healthiest people, are those that can withstand discomfort. Just as muscles need resistance to grow stronger, minds need challenge to mature. Political correctness was meant to protect dignity, but overprotection—even of feelings— can quietly stunt development. Shielding children from every controversial idea leaves them unprepared for a world that will not always agree with them.

We can—and must—restore balance. Teaching empathy in speech is vital; teaching endurance in conversation is equally so. The goal is not to abandon careful language but to pair it with courage. Children should learn that they can listen to words they dislike without losing their worth, and that they can speak their truth respectfully even when others disagree.

Parents and educators can model this by demonstrating calm curiosity instead of outrage. When someone uses an outdated term, instead of shaming, we can explain. When a student expresses an unpopular opinion, instead of silencing, we can encourage an open dialogue. Correcting with compassion keeps communication alive.

Political correctness at its best teaches kindness. At its worst, it teaches fear. The difference lies in intent—whether we are trying to help others grow or simply trying to avoid being uncomfortable ourselves. The next generation needs to see that civility and honesty are not enemies; they are partners in progress.

If we want children to become strong thinkers and resilient communicators, we must encourage speech that is both mindful and brave. Words should build bridges, not walls. And when we teach them that the answer to offense is not silence but dialogue, we give them something more powerful than correctness—we give them connection.

Closing Thoughts

The Gift of Resilience

If you've read this far, it means you care deeply — about your children, your students, and the kind of world they will inherit. That care is the foundation of everything good in parenting and teaching.

The truth is, we've all done our best with the information we had. The shift toward protecting children emotionally came from love, not laziness. But now, we know more. We can see that overprotection, however well-intentioned, has left many children underprepared for real life.

Resilience is not a trait we are born with; it's a gift we earn through experience—and one of the greatest gifts we can pass on. Every time a child learns to calm themselves, face fear, or recover from disappointment, they gain strength that no one can take away. It is the quiet, steady confidence that says, I can handle life, even when it's hard.

In a culture that often confuses comfort with happiness, our challenge as adults is to reintroduce the value of struggle. Struggle does not mean suffering; it means growth. It's the process of turning uncertainty into understanding and mistakes into wisdom. Shielding children from every hardship doesn't protect them—it limits them. They cannot discover their strength if they are never allowed to use it.

True resilience is not about ignoring feelings. It's about acknowledging them and moving forward anyway. It's the bridge between emotion and action, empathy and endurance. When children learn that uncomfortable emotions are survivable, they stop fearing them. They realize that pain can coexist with progress, and that disappointment can live beside hope.

The ultimate goal of parenting, teaching, and mentoring is not to create children who never fall—it's to raise adults who know how to rise. We can remind them that failure is feedback, that challenges are invitations, and that character is built most deeply in the moments when no one is watching.

When we raise resilient children, we also heal ourselves. We begin to let go of the fear that every setback will break them. We rediscover the joy of watching them succeed because they struggled, not in spite of it. And we strengthen our families, our schools, and our communities in the process.

Resilience doesn't erase hardship—it transforms it. It's the steady voice inside that whispers, "You can handle this." And when we help children find that voice, we give them something more lasting than comfort: we give them courage.

That is the true gift of resilience—and the legacy every generation deserves to inherit.

So, let's keep listening, keep guiding, and most of all, keep believing that strength and compassion are not opposites — they're partners.

Together, they build people — and a society — that can stand through anything.

About the Author

Jennifer Topping is a wife, parent, and advocate for raising emotionally strong and resilient children in today's world. Drawing from years of observation, conversation, and reflection on modern family life, she writes with warmth and clarity about the importance of balance—between empathy and accountability, understanding and endurance.

Her goal is to help parents, educators, and communities rediscover the values that build true strength in children: responsibility, perseverance, and self-awareness. *The Coping Deficit: How Overprotection Broke Resilience* is both her call to reflection and her message of hope—a reminder that it's never too late to raise a generation capable of facing life with confidence and grace.

www.ingramcontent.com/pod-product-compliance
Lightning Source LLC
Chambersburg PA
CBHW030525130626
46549CB00007B/3103